THEY HE SHE HE ME

by maya & matthew

Free to Be!

Text © 2017 by Maya and Matthew Smith-Gonzalez
Art Copyright © 2017 by Maya Christina Gonzalez
Published by Reflection Press, San Francisco, CA

Reflection Press is an independent publisher of radical and revolutionary children's books and works that expand cultural and spiritual awareness. **www.reflectionpress.com**

All rights reserved. Printed in the USA
ISBN 978-1-945289-06-4 (hardcover)
ISBN 978-1-945289-09-5 (paperback)
Library of Congress Control Number: 2017913263
Book Design by Matthew SG
The Gender Wheel® books support The Gender Wheel Curriculum,
a holistic, nature-based approach to understanding gender.
www.genderwheel.com

For permissions, bulk orders, or if you receive defective or
misprinted books, please contact us at info@reflectionpress.com

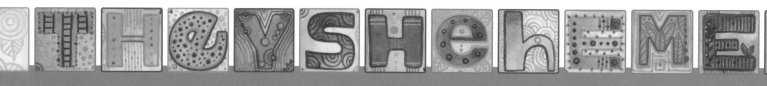

for Zai & Sky,
may you always be free!
– M+M

Reflection Press, San Francisco, CA

Free to Be!

Me   Me   Me

Me   Me   Me

Me   Me   Me

Me   Me   Me

He   He   He

He   He   He

He   He   He

He   He   He

She   She   She

She   She   She

She   She   She

She   She   She

They   They   They

They   They   They

They   They   They

They   They   They

Tree   Ze   Tree

Ze   Tree   Ze

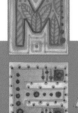

Pronouns

When you were born you were given a name, and a pronoun,
probably *he* or *she*.

As you get older and know yourself more and more on the inside
some of the ideas of *she* and *he* may fit you
and some of them may not.

Ideas about *he* and *she* are very strong right now.

Many people believe *HE* means ONLY certain things
and *SHE* means ONLY certain things.

These ideas affect what people think about everything.
How you dress, how you wear your hair or how you express the
spirit of who you are, even what colors you like.

People can think they know what
your pronoun is based on their
ideas about *she* and *he*.

This is a way of only looking at the
outside of a person and not the
inside of a person.

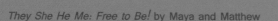

They She He Me: Free to Be! by Maya and Matthew

Freeing Pronouns

On the inside,
you may not feel like *he* or *she* at all, maybe
they feels the most free, or you may feel
like both *she* and *he*.

But mostly, you probably just feel like *yourself*.

This inside part is the most important part because
there is no one else like you in the world.
This is why everyone should be free to be exactly who they are
on the inside!

Who you are is not always something you can put into words
or explain. You just know who you are because you are!

Pronouns can be a way to share how you feel on the inside.
Because this inside part is the most important part of you,
it cannot be about outside ideas of how people think *she* or
he is 'supposed' to act. It has to be about how you feel.

The truth is ideas about *he* and *she* change all the
time. If they don't fit, you might be an important
part of changing them.

They She He Me: Free to Be! by Maya and Matthew

Claiming Pronouns

Because there is only one you,
only you can know you.

That means there is never a right or wrong way to be you,
only your way.

This is also why only you can know what pronoun expresses the spirit
of who you are on the inside.

And why being free to claim the pronoun or pronouns that feel right
to you is important.

You know what feels right to you both inside and outside.

You can even have an inside pronoun
and an outside pronoun.

They She He Me: Free to Be! by Maya and Matthew

Creating Pronouns

Not only can *he* and *she* mean more than what people think, there are also more pronouns than just *she* and *he*.

You are not alone if *he* and *she* don't fit. Many people have played with pronouns and still do because of how they feel inside.

Here are some ideas.

You can use *your own name* as your pronoun.

You can change pronouns from *he* to *she* or from *she* to *he*,

you can use new ones like *ze*

or create your own like *tree*!

Some people use *they* which is a perfect way.

There are many more pronouns waiting to be discovered and used.

People are creating new pronouns all the time!

Using Pronouns

To begin creating room for everyone including yourself, there are ways to use pronouns that make room for more than just *she* and *he*.

When you first meet someone tell them your name and you can ask theirs. You don't have to know more than that to play!

If you hear a pronoun from that person--great, you can use that pronoun. If you don't hear a pronoun from that person and you need to use one--you could use *they* and keep playing. And maybe *they* is what they love to be called anyway!

And what about you? Do you like to be called *they* too? You could share your pronoun by saying it plain and simple if you want or you could just stick with your name.
Do what feels right to you.

Doing things like this lets people

know that you have bigger ideas about *he* and *she* and you know there are more than two pronouns and ways of being yourself in the world. This helps everyone feel freer and more welcome to play.

Playing with Pronouns

If you want to keep playing with as many people as possible and making room for yourself, keep playing with pronouns!

You can practice seeing more of the inside of people and not just the outside of people. Use your imagination to play with how characters in movies and books could feel on the inside.

Begin by using *they* for different characters. Or change a main character from *he* to *she* or from *she* to *he*. You don't have to change their name, just their pronoun. Playing like this gives you even bigger ideas about *he* and *she* and gives you bigger ideas about how people feel on the inside, including you.

Keep claiming! Keep playing!
Keep knowing yourself
inside and outside.
You rock!

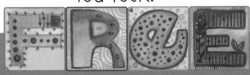

About M+M

Hi!

We hope you had fun through our book. This is the first one we've officially written together. There weren't a lot of words, but it was Matthew's idea and Maya's art. Then Maya wrote the story in the back with Matthew close by.

Together we're partners and parents of our fabulous kids! We make our books for them. When Maya was born she was given the pronoun *she* and since it mostly fits she kept it for now but inside feels like much more than what we usually think of as *she*. When Matthew was born he was given the pronoun *she* but came to understand that *he* represented the truest part of him, inside and out.

We talk about things like this all the time, but it makes a big difference to have a book to hold. It makes it easier to have conversations and look at everything more closely. This is why we want to share our book with you.

As parents we want our kids to feel fully free to blossom into their maximum magnificence. We also want our kids to understand our 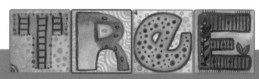 family and the fabulous people in our lives. Us, Matthew's dads, both sides of our gorgeous chosen family and friends! We're all part of the LGBTQI community with lots of ways to be *he, she, they* and much more!

We want there to be lots of room for all kids to play and be free to be themselves. We think books are a great place for us all to meet and begin playing.

See you again soon!

xomaya and matthew

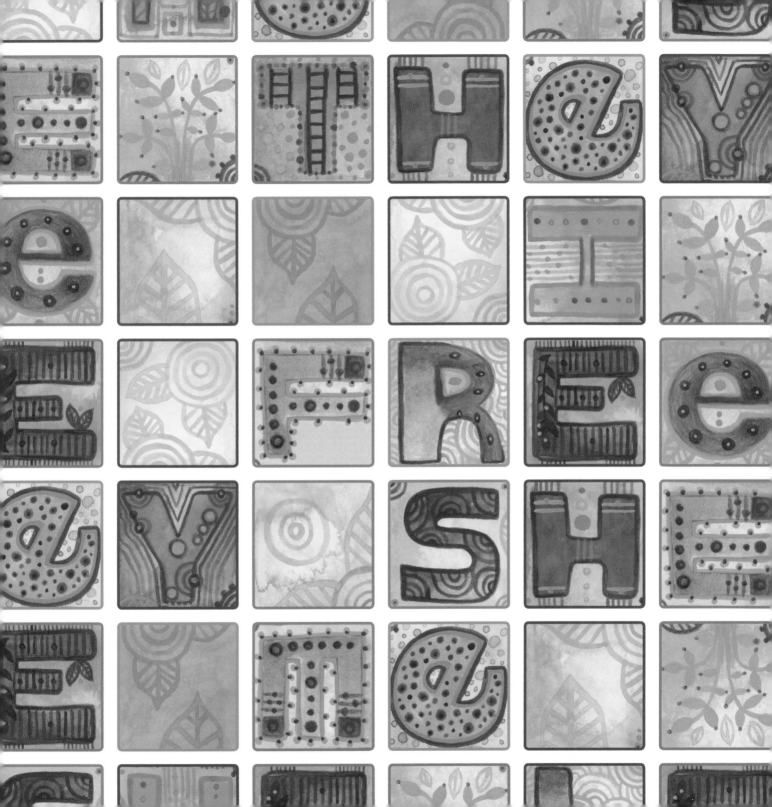

for the Grown-Ups

Being familiar and confident about the material for yourself makes a big difference when sharing it with kids. What that means is looking at your own ideas about gender in an honest and open way to see what assumptions and stereotypes you may hold. Many of your ideas and beliefs about gender may have been taken on without you knowing it. This is an opportunity to look at them with awareness and a larger perspective. Being able to see through your thinking also helps you see how language is used in relation to gender. This puts you in a stronger position to make choices that expand and free gender and welcome as many people to play as possible.

Being Comfortable with the unknown and ambiguity

<u>In the book:</u> Note that the kids in this book are just a small sampling of the many fabulous ways that people express who they are inside and outside. There are literally infinite more!

The kids in the book are shown in fun, playful ways and kids reading the book may recognize their friends, family or their selves in the imagery.

Consider looking at it without reading the pronouns first so that kids feel free to relate and associate with who they want without judgment or expectations. Then look at it again reading the pronouns and model being curious and open about what pronouns each kid in the book claims as their own.

Notice what kids from the *ME* pages show up with other pronouns. Notice what kids don't claim more pronouns than *ME*. Did you find the kid who identifies as both *he* and *she*?

<u>Out in the world:</u> There is a strong compulsion to categorize and define in Western culture, including people. Many well intentioned folks unconsciously reaffirm gender stereotypes and assumptions even as they are trying to dismantle them to be more inclusive. As the grown-up you have the powerful position of being able to model an alternative as you become more aware and engaged with ideas about gender.

Notice that the words *girl* and *boy* are not used in the text for kids. This is intentional. By providing other ways to think and navigate the world beyond these words, the text naturally helps to dismantle and redirect away from assumptions and stereotypes. This opens up and helps develop new ways of thinking and looking at the world.

You can show that it's OK not to 'know' someone's gender or pronoun out in the world and still engage or play with them. Don't make a point of it or a big deal. In fact the more casual and normal you can be about it the better. This normalizing speaks volumes. It is through your nonverbal behavior that you communicate your intent the strongest.

Read over the kids section and take the lead in modeling the suggestions yourself. Notice if there are places where you feel stuck or lose your words. Go slowly. Remember your intention is what's important. Learning is a normal part of life for grown-ups too.

Expanding Yourself, Expanding the World for our kids

One of the most valuable things you can do to contribute to dismantling the binary and supporting full gender inclusion is to become aware of your own assumptions. Are you calling people who wear dresses she? Or calling people with short hair and pants he? The more you can break down all assumptions connected to gender the easier it will be to free assumptions about everybody! This includes looking at everything, especially how you speak and how you encourage kids in your life to speak.

Using gender neutral words as much as possible is key. Consider how to use *parent*, instead of mother or father. *Sibling*, instead of brother or sister. *Our kid*, instead of daughter or son. *Kid*, instead of boy or girl. And so on. This is especially important during the first five years. It not only provides freedom for a growing child to be who they are, it also sets precedence for ways of thinking and using language that are inclusive. This is less about changing all the names of everything and more about modeling the existence of all gender possibilities equally.

Making change can feel uncomfortable at first, especially if it feels like loss. Expanding yourself to see your assumptions and take different actions can feel empowering, but speaking out and holding perspectives that others don't see yet can feel challenging. This is especially true if you're not used to speaking out. Different emotions will come up for different people. It helps to maintain a larger perspective about gender and the real effects gender inequality in all its many manifestations has on our culture. Remember the very real life of our kids and how gender affects them and even you. The more aware and confident you become in yourself and your understanding of gender assumptions and stereotypes in real life, the easier all this will be. Maintaining a larger perspective at the same time helps you stay committed as you are growing into your knowing.

What it takes to make real change

Having one book, one lesson, one moment can make a difference, but the binary of *he/she* is very dominant right now and can easily eclipse any alternative. If you want to have a significant impact you must maintain a consistent and persistent perspective that a kid can easily adopt and use because it makes sense to them. To do this a kid literally must hear you provide pronoun alternatives everyday in as many ways as possible.

This means constancy and creativity. What can you realistically maintain? Perhaps you convert to using *they* for most pronouns. Or have a set of books that you always read with different pronouns or particular movies that you always look at in gender expansive ways.

You can use this book to relate to specific characters in other books and movies. Look and see if one of the pronoun book characters reminds you of a character in another book if they used *he* instead of *she*. Can you find one that reminds you of a character if they used *they* or *ze* instead of *he* or *she*? What changes about them? Anything? Everything? Be playful and curious. Imagine the freedom these characters might experience if their gender was fluid. You may not have imagined how much freedom you discover for yourself and your kids when gender stereotypes and assumptions are loosened or even lifted!

Building and Reclaiming

It's revolutionary when you and yours can see beyond the gender binary of *he* and *she*. Holding perspectives like this can put you in the position of ambassador as you negotiate the world. Sports teams, schools, public bathrooms, clothing departments, colors, haircuts, even playgrounds and family. Many places use *he* and *she* to categorize and separate people and even behaviors. You can maintain larger perspectives by making a habit of including non-binary stories alongside the dominant *he*, *she* ones. As small of a step as this may seem it makes a difference and vibrates out in ways you may not be able to see. Every step counts. Many people in the LGBTQI community already maintain perspectives like this in their lives. You can too even if you or your kids are not part of the community. Respectfully expanding gender inclusion means modeling it ourselves first and foremost, and including it as a natural part of our social justice work and awareness. Taking the time to support change beyond the binary creates a more welcoming and inclusive world for everyone. You rock!

Singular *They* - Yes, it's grammatically correct

Read more: www.merriam-webster.com/words-at-play/singular-nonbinary-they

More Books

by Maya Gonzalez:

Claiming Face: Self-Empowerment Through Self-Portraiture, Educator's Guide

Gender Now Coloring Book, A Learning Adventure for Children and Adults

The Gender Wheel: a Story about Bodies and Gender For Every Body

They, She, He easy as ABC *(companion to They She He Me)*

Call Me Tree/Llámame árbol *(pronoun free)*
See Maya's Note to Readers: www.genderwheel.com/tree

by Others:

What Makes a Baby
by Cory Silverberg, illustrated by Fiona Smyth

Stacey's Not a Girl
by Colt Keo-Meier, illustrated by Jesse Yang

Sam!
by Dani Gabriel, illustrated by Robert Liu-Trujillo

One of a Kind, Like Me/ Único como yo
by Laurin Mayeno, illustrated by Robert Liu-Trujillo

They Call Me Mix/ Me llaman maestre
by Lourdes Rivas, illustrated by Breena Nuñez

Is That for a Boy or a Girl?
by S. Bear Bergman, illustrated by Rachel Dougherty

The Boy and the Bindi
by Vivek Shraya, illustrated by Rajni Perera

Educational Tools & Games!

PlayingWithPronouns.com

Gender inclusive educational card deck inspired by this book!

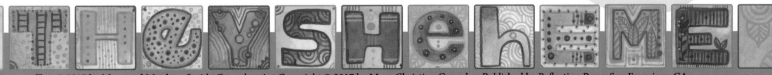

Text © 2017 by Maya and Matthew Smith-Gonzalez, Art Copyright © 2017 by Maya Christina Gonzalez, Published by Reflection Press, San Francisco, CA
For permissions, bulk orders, or if you receive defective or misprinted books, please contact us at info@reflectionpress.com

CPSIA information can be obtained at www.ICGtesting.com
Printed in the USA
LVIW010222250321
682396LV00001B/1